D1456112

I've been blessed with a wonderful and loving family, which includes my parents, a twin brother, three children and their spouses, and four exciting grandchildren. I've also, for the major portion of my lifetime, had the advantage of sharing my joys and sorrows with devoted and loving friends. This book is dedicated to the following dear people: Marilyn and Joel Sprayregen, who exhibit a rare combination of intelligence and guts. Regardless of what hand I was dealt, they were always there to back me up.

Ellen Elmaleh, a gal of great courage, integrity, and wonderment.

Arlene and Walter Meranze . . . From laughter to tears, and back to laughter, our paths crisscross, but our souls are always together.

Our sincere appreciation to the following individuals and organizations: Robert Carney, *Golf Digest;* Mel Cowher; Paul Chung, Paul Chung Literary Agency; James Clearwater; Nicholas Granat; Brooks Johnson; David Karmin; George Peper, *Golf Magazine*; Peter Pliterris and the staff at Nikon Electronic Imaging; Tony Sclafani, Romantic Travel; Mark Serota; Peter Sorenson; our editors at Gramercy Books/Random House Value Publishing; Eric Weissman; and Rick Wester.

Special thanks to our dearest friend and "soul mate," Bill Hallberg, for his continued faith, support, wisdom, enthusiasm, and caring.

Grateful acknowledgment is given to the following sources for a number of the short quotes in this book: *Beyond the Fairway* by Jeff Wallach; *Golf's Golden Grind* by Al Berkow; *The First Coming* by John Feinstein; *Tiger* by John Strege; *Dormie One* by Holworthy Hall; *The Year of Getting to Know Me* by Ethan Canin; and *Links* by Lorne Rubenstein.

The Soul of Tiger Woods

God gave me a gift. And he trusted me to take care of it.

Earl Woods

The Soul of Tiger Woods

Gerald Sprayregen

Foreword and Additional Text by

William Hallberg

Design by

Vicki Sylvester

GRAMERCY BOOKS
New York

This 1998 edition is published by Gramercy Books,™
an imprint of Random House Value Publishing, Inc.,
201 East 50th Street, New York, New York 10022.

Gramercy Books™ and design are trademarks of
Random House Value Publishing, Inc.

Random House
New York • Toronto • London • Sydney • Auckland
http://www.randomhouse.com/

Printed in the United States of America. Bound in Mexico.

The Soul of Tiger Woods is not a publication authorized by Tiger Woods, the PGA,
or their representatives or related enterprises.

A CIP catalog record for this book is available from the Library of Congress.

ISBN 0-517-20458-4

8 7 6 5 4 3 2 1

The Soul of Tiger Woods has been a strange odyssey for me. Golf, until recently, has not been a sport that tugged at my heartstrings. Many years ago, my passions in college, besides romancing beautiful coeds, were baseball, basketball, and tennis. But recently, the beauty and elegance of The Masters, coupled with the raw power and romance of Pebble Beach, California, have kindled a spark in my tennis-oriented heart—a spark that continues to flicker.

The idea for The Soul of Tiger Woods was created in a meeting in New York in July of 1997, when Vicki Sylvester, my partner and designer, and I gave birth to a concept of a series of sports books that would attempt to delve into the souls of the individuals. Tiger had already won The Masters in April, and he was "hot, hot, hot"! We decided that our first book would be The Soul of Tiger Woods, and hopefully, it would be something more than just a series of attractive images of a handsome young athlete. It was our intention to produce a book that would have a unique collection of thought-provoking images and quotations. Within a few days, Vicki and I were on a plane to Scotland, for the British Open, to photograph this "wee laddie," who at the age of twenty-one had become a household name around the globe as well as a media sensation.

I have been running ever since. As Tiger has followed the sun, I have followed the Tiger; from Houston to Orlando, from New York to Spain, from Pebble Beach to Las Vegas. Along the fairways, I have met and spoken with Earl Woods, Tiger's father, who remains the dominant driving force in his son's life; for this reason, we have devoted a portion of our book to the relationship of fathers and sons. It is the key to Tiger and the theme of our book. I have also spent a number of hours with Mike Cowan—"Fluff"—the quintessential caddy, who has become a celebrity in his own right. The third member of "team Tiger" is the warm and engaging Butch Harmon, Tiger's coach, with whom I have managed to have a few brief conversations between practice rounds. Aside from eye contact, Tiger and I have never met.

Over the past year, in my attempt to try to understand this all-consuming passion that infiltrates the minds and souls of millions of golfers, I have read more than seventy books on golf—wonderful books written by gifted authors. However, there was one book, The Soul of Golf by William Hallberg, that touched my soul. The warmth, wit, caring, and gentleness of Bill flowed from his pen onto the page and then into my heart. When it was decided many months later that we needed a collaborator on The Soul of Tiger Woods, Bill Hallberg became our obvious choice, and shortly thereafter he became our adviser and dear friend.

Please jump into your golf cart, and join us on a tour of the soul of Tiger Woods.

Gerald Sprayregen

Tiger Woods is perhaps the most photographed of all contemporary golfers, in part because the camera likes him better than any player since Palmer. Popular as he was in his heyday, Jack Nicklaus never quite related to the lens of a camera, which too often captured him as either grumpy or merely studious. Palmer, with his crow's feet, pursed lips, and cocked head, was another story altogether; he was a perpetual photograph just waiting to be taken.

Woods, like Palmer, is an infinitely more available photographic subject than, say, a basketball star like Michael Jordan who plays in arenas where cameras are forbidden to the average fan. Golf is an open-air event staged over five or six days—if one includes practice rounds and pro-ams, when anybody with a point-and-shoot can take snapshots of their hero. When the actual golf tournament begins, though, only professionals are allowed to photograph the players.

This is where Gerald Sprayregen comes in. If you are among the gallery at tee-off time and you see a man hanging from the scaffolding of a TV tower or standing on the hood of a cop car, chances are it's Sprayregen, getting that hard-fought image. He will do absolutely anything to get a shot that is insightful, original, and artful. The fact is that most of the images produced by professionals, those that find their way into golf periodicals and coffee-table books, are less artful than Sprayregen's images and are simply illustrative. On the other hand, the photography in Gerald Sprayregen's *The Soul of Tiger Woods* distinguishes itself from those popular magazines and glossy tomes. Sprayregen's images humanize Tiger Woods, capturing him at ease, off-guard and vulnerable. We see him under the heavy gaze of adoring fans, or behind a microphone, alone with his dad, besieged by kids with pens and programs. The perspective here is unfailingly original, wonderfully idiosyncratic, and always more knowable than the cliches to which we've become accustomed. Gerry brings the heart and soul of an artist to his task, but it is his unfaltering eye for the essential truth of a moment that gives his images such uncommon brilliance. Here we see the real Tiger Woods, in all his manifestations, completely human and totally real.

When Tiger Woods won the 1997 Masters by a dozen strokes, I for one shuddered in awe, admiration, and *fear*. His dismantling of the hallowed Augusta fairways, not to mention his competition, was so utterly convincing that I actually believed that this kid would win every tournament he entered, turning professional golf on its ear for years to come. I also trembled in contemplation of the cultural influence someone so prodigiously talented and charismatic might exert. I comforted myself with TV images of Michael Jordan hawking underwear and Nike shoes and beverages and Wheaties; after all, the earth hasn't flipped off its axis as a result of his influences, although our buying patterns and cultural attitudes have surely been altered—sometimes for the best. But what about Tiger? Could he present himself to the public with the grace and identifiable morality (ubiquitous commerciality notwithstanding) as his fellow sports icon Michael Jordan?

There are obvious cultural benefits to the appearance of a young, elegant man of color on the landscape of a sport so predictable in its conservatism, exclusivity—and whiteness. Tiger Woods is by no means the first African-American player to tee it up on the PGA tour. Calvin Peete had his days in the sun, and Jim Thorpe was a significant player in the 1980s. Prior to that, there were Charlie Sifford and Lee Elder. Nevertheless, golf has in essence been the affluent suburban flip side to modern-day basketball, a sport adopted enthusiastically by inner-city and rural kids, a sport played on asphalt courts in urban parks and dusty patches of farmyard next to barns in rural America. So, there's nothing particularly jarring about a Michael Jordan's stardom in the realm of hoops nor his success as a cultural icon with basketball as his platform. But, let's face it: whereas Jordan is an icon, Woods is an iconoclast.

There has been resistance, subtle and overt, to Tiger's splashy arrival on the golfing scene. His fellow professionals have complained of cockiness, aloofness, temper, and every species of frailty imaginable. Some of their criticisms are at times valid; some are born of jealousy and resentment. However, it is the raw humanity that Tiger Woods projects onto a staid, highly choreographed sport that has popularized him. He's no saint, nor is he the unchallenged golfing god we hoped (or feared) he might be. He's less superhuman than *hyperhuman*, an emblem of ourselves in a game that, more than any other, mirrors the ups and downs of our daily lives.

What Sprayregen's wonderful images capture is not only the artistry of a rare golfer of singular skills, but a young man more like us than we'd care to admit. Now, at last, we get to know him.

William Hallberg

TIGER WOODS!

TIGER WOODS!

TIGER WOODS!

Scribbled on a hat in ink,

in pencil on a program,

in crayon on a mustard-covered paper plate.

Tiger Woods!

Tiger Woods!

Just one more, and then another . . . and another.

An obligation of the trade for some who sign their names

and fight to keep their train of thought

for battles yet ahead.

William Hallberg

"**You da man**," *they shout.* "**You da man, Tiger.**"

The phrase rolls across the green terrain.

Years ago, other men cast their legendary shadows on much humbler fairways,

men unknown to most of us who love the game. Rhodes, Elder, Sifford, and Thorpe.

Pioneers who persevered and paved the way.

Now the man who strides the emerald fairways, illuminated by a brilliant sun,

is master of a sport so long denied to men like him until its own emancipation.

William Hallberg

I've learned

to trust

the subconscious.

My instincts

have never lied

to me.

Tiger Woods

There are no fans with periscopes,

nor cameramen,

nor hot dog stands,

nor humping dogs,

nor Cessnas trailing ads

for pizzas—TWO FOR ONE!

You've made a tunnel for yourself

and gone inside to think:

downhill,

left to right,

slick as an eel.

Aim high and merely

tap the thing;

then let fate take hold of it . . .

AND WAIT.

William Hallberg

I have so much

admiration

for this kid.

Tiger

is one of my idols.

I am in awe

of what

he's done.

Michael Jordan

A golf spectator
is satisfied
when he gets to see,
at least a few times
during the course
of his long day,
a ball struck with
consummate power
and amazing control;
a ball sent soaring
from a standing start,
then floating to earth
and stopping within
a prescribed
swatch of lawn.
It is an awesome sensation,
not unlike watching
a rocket launch.

Al Berkow

Golf is a trip.
In many weathers,
inner and outer,
amid many a green
and winding landscape,
I have asked myself what
the peculiar bliss
of this demanding game is,
a bliss that at times threatens
to relegate all the rest of life . . .
to the shadows.

I *am curiously,*
disproportionately,
undeservedly
happy
on a golf course,
and perhaps
we are all here
for much the same
reason.

John Updike
Addressing the U.S. Golf Association
on its 100th anniversary

On a picturesque mountainside oasis in Spain called **Valderrama**,

a battle was waged to determine the supremacy of golfers

who are divided by the mighty Atlantic.

For four days, the battle raged on, as the doughboys, **led by Kite and Woods,**

went head to head against the fearless ensemble of **Ballesteros, Montgomery, and company.**

When the last putt had been holed, and the last flag had been replaced,

it was the European cartel who toasted the Ryder Cup with champagne and joyous laughter.

Gerald Sprayregen

In my own mind, I'm always the favorite ...

It's not surprising if you win when you have your mind set

from the start of the week that you're going to win.

Tiger Woods

His club

came back in the long, graceful arc
that even his fellow pros envy,
and then it came down,
whipping through the hitting area
with such force that the nearby grandstand
seemed likely to start shaking.
The ball climbed into the sky,
becoming a tiny dot against the fluffy clouds overhead;
it hung there while all the spectators gaped,
and then it came down 290 yards away.

John Feinstein

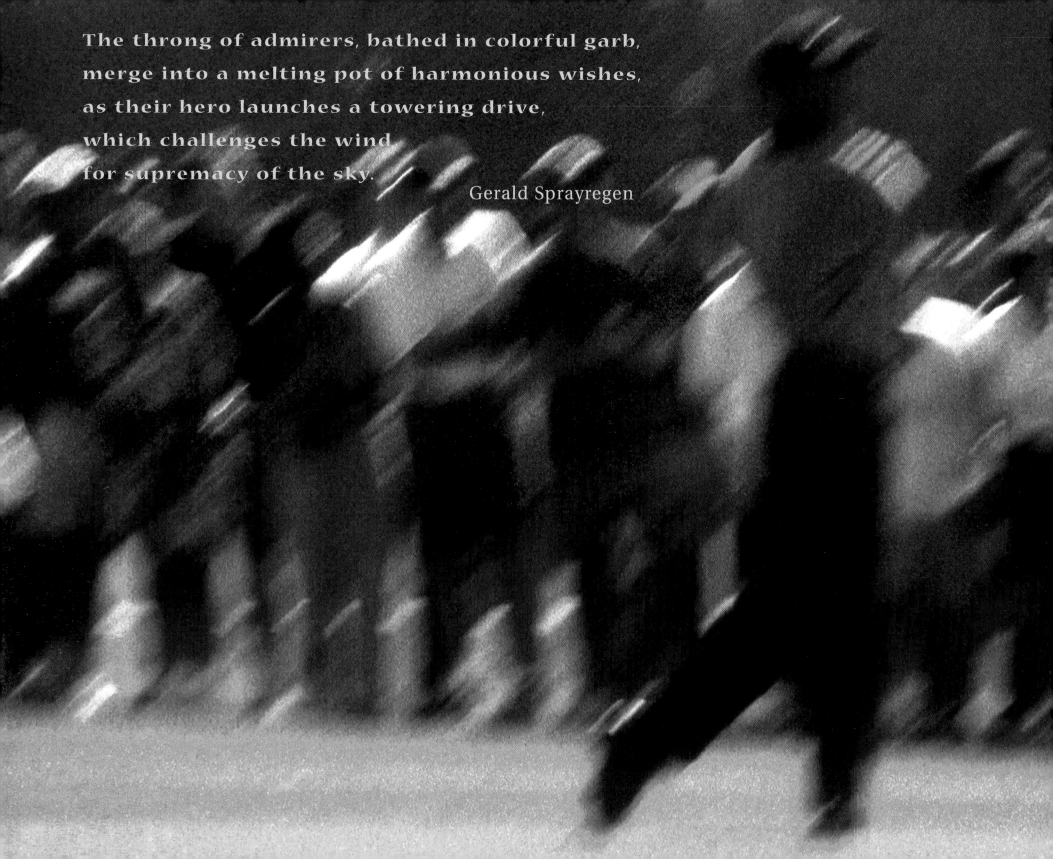

The throng of admirers, bathed in colorful garb,
merge into a melting pot of harmonious wishes,
as their hero launches a towering drive,
which challenges the wind
for supremacy of the sky.

Gerald Sprayregen

"I would like to see him acknowledge the gallery more."

"I don't think he's having fun."

"He looks uptight."

A golfer needs to be in touch
with the people who pay
to see him play.

Lee Elder

GOLF

may be

a sophisticated game.

At least,

it is usually played

with the countenance

of great dignity.

It is, nevertheless, a

GAME

OF

considerable

PASSION,

either of the explosive type,

or that which burns inwardly

AND

wears the

SOUL.

Bobby Jones

The overpowering beauty of a Masters morning consumes the souls

of the thousands who tread upon its hallowed ground.

They are here to see Arnie, Jack, Tom, Tiger, and others,

but it is the haunting memories of the past

that bring them back year after year.

The memories of the azaleas in full bloom, the mirrored ponds,

and the massive trees silhouetted against the manicured carpeted greens

make even the quintessential game of golf

a mere backdrop to nature's wonders.

Gerald Sprayregen

I want to be the best there ever was . . .

I want to be the Michael Jordan of golf.

Tiger Woods

He's so long, he reduces the course
to nothing, absolutely nothing.

Jack Nicklaus
Speaking of Tiger's historic victory at
The Masters in Augusta, 1997

For most of us,
golf is just a symbol.

The greens and traps and fairways

are mere arenas where we allow ourselves

to grieve or rejoice at our mortality.

The futility of the buried lie,

the infinite promise of a splendid drive

posing in the middle of the fairway,

the frustration of a putt that pulls up shy . . .

they're all about something beyond ourselves.

But for the soul who earns his bread

by digging roughs and sinking putts,

the symbol is an absolute

that stares him in the eye.

William Hallberg

Someday my dad will not be out here with me.

Someday I won't even be able to call him

from a scrubby, unknown golf course

out in the strange universe—

as I've done from Texas and Idaho and Thailand—

to tell him I just sunk my first eagle,

or broke my own personal best,

and to hear his pride in me.

But even then, even when I'm alone in the world
in a way that all men must eventually be alone
in the world—without a father—
he'll know when I've played well,
because my dad will always be someplace
inside of my swing.

Jeff Wallach

It's said,
"The child is father to the man,"

*and there
are times
when this
is so.
Sons,
in truth,
regret
that
poignant
moment
of their lives
when roles
reverse*

**and fathers
lose their power to command the day.**

Thus,
on those rare green afternoons

when time

dissolves

and sons

are able

to resume their

deferential

ways,

there's joy

in any

moment

when a father

finds the

tender means
to find himself a father once again.

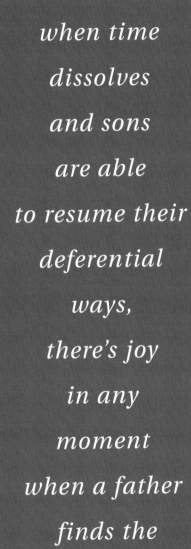

William Hallberg

In a sense,

Tiger is hunting

neither trophies nor money,

though he is certain

to accumulate

a warehouse full of each.

He is hunting big game,

the Golden Bear, Jack Nicklaus.

A man will measure

each of his achievements

against those of Nicklaus,

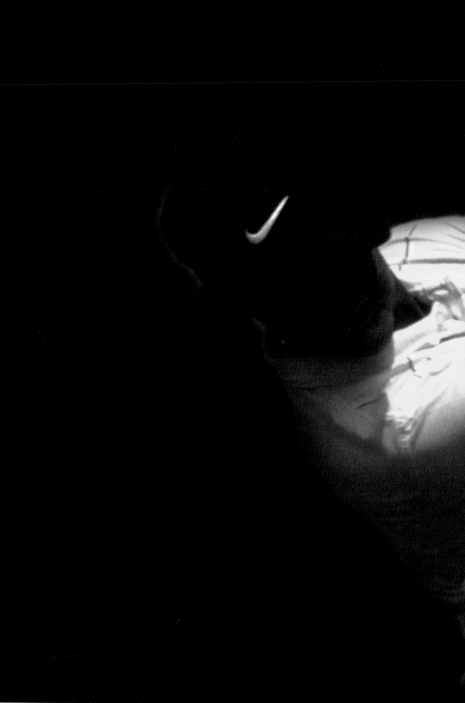

who is recognized

as the greatest player

in history—

the same title

to which

Tiger aspires.

To wrest it from him,

he will have

to systematically

trump each installment

on Nicklaus's record.

John Strege

Indeed, from the inception of the finals . . .

the boy had shown himself considerate and generous,

quick of applause and slow of alibi,

a dashing, brilliant, dangerous golfer

with the fire of an adventurer and the grace of a cavalier.

He was confident yet modest.

He was dogged while he smiled . . .

but the smile faded and vanished

only when he saw that Hargrave was in difficulty.

The gallery, nine-tenths of it, was with him boisterously.

The gallery was frankly

on the side of youth and spontaneity.

Holworthy Hall

A golf ball at rest gleams with opportunity.

Its innocent dimples and alabaster skin

promise absolute submission

to your every whim.

Never trust a golf ball.

It was conceived to betray

your keenest calculations and

will do its level best to make you the fool.

In an artist's hands,
the golf club
is a paintbrush,
whose marks
upon a canvas
speak of mastering
a landscape . . .
and judiciousness . . .
and subtle strokes
so spare that one
would hardly know
that he was ever there.
Until, that is,
we see the product
of his work,
and thrill
at what he's done.

William Hallberg

But so close together
that the two of you are nearly one.
You close your eyes and count the clicks
of club heads knocking.
Two hundred clicks, three hundred yards.
At this moment, golf is beautiful
and clean and comprehensible.

William Hallberg

It's easy to love golf when it loves you back.

Imagine walking through
the dappled sunlight
of the final fairway,
your arm around your caddy, Fluff,
relieved and happy
at the day's success.
Your shadows lie before you,
yours and his, side by side,
his shorter and wider than your own.

The snap of Fluff's lighter, the burning of cigarette paper,
a whiff of smoke . . . are all a comfort to a golfer
when the world beyond the fairways is an abstraction
at best.

Fluff. An odd name for a man
on whom the force of gravity exerts such a pull.
A cannonball of a man, weighted down by iron tools,
pauses now and then
to blow evanescent smoke into the weightless air.

The smoke tells a caddy something.
The wind is left to right.
The wind is in our faces.
A hovering plume suggests a calm
that simplifies calculations.

William Hallberg

This caddy is a Renaissance man.

*Part psychoanalyst,
part beast of burden, part physicist,
part mother hen.*

He's superhuman, too.

*He'll change the wind's direction
for "his man,"
or part the water
(or walk on it, if required);*

**he can will a golf ball
back on course,
or wish it in the hole.**

William Hallberg

My world

has redefined itself,

down to one hole,

a few trees, and

a small amount of sky,

where the light-gray mist

hides the painted face

of morning,

and I alone

will determine

my own destiny.

Gerald Sprayregen

There is no shot in golf that Woods doesn't think he can pull off. *That is part of his greatness . . .*

Tiger Woods is nothing if not bold.
At times he goes beyond bold to reckless ...

John Feinstein

Silver brooms of morning grass sweep skyward, windblown.
An elegant backdrop for the finest sporting motion known to man,
the driving of the ball.

William Hallberg

*E*scape with me,

past the horizons

into the tomorrows.

Gerald Sprayregen

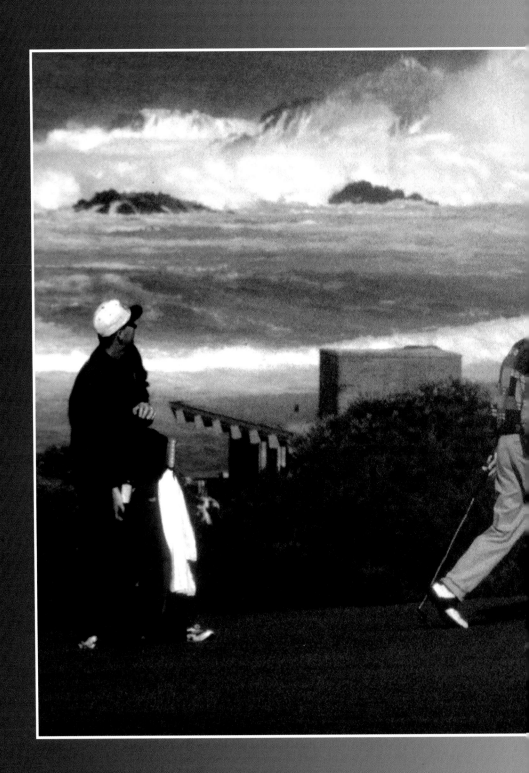

Golf *is 20 percent mechanics and technique. The other 80 percent is philosophy, humor, tragedy,*

romance,

melodrama, companionship,
camaraderie, cussedness,
and conversation.

Grantland Rice, 1920

The warm current breezes

filter through the canyons of spectators,

as our day of glory approaches.

Elongated shadows,

cast by the mighty oaks,

assure the assault of evening.

We are two athletes,

my shaft and I,

muted together by countless hours

of rehearsals,

which have transformed

us into a coalition of one.

Gerald Sprayregen

He stands alone,

warmed only by the fading sun and the promise of adventure.

A God-given talent, brains, courage, beauty,

and the soul of a warrior

are his birthrights.

Will he rewrite history,

or simply be

another paragraph?

Gerald Sprayregen

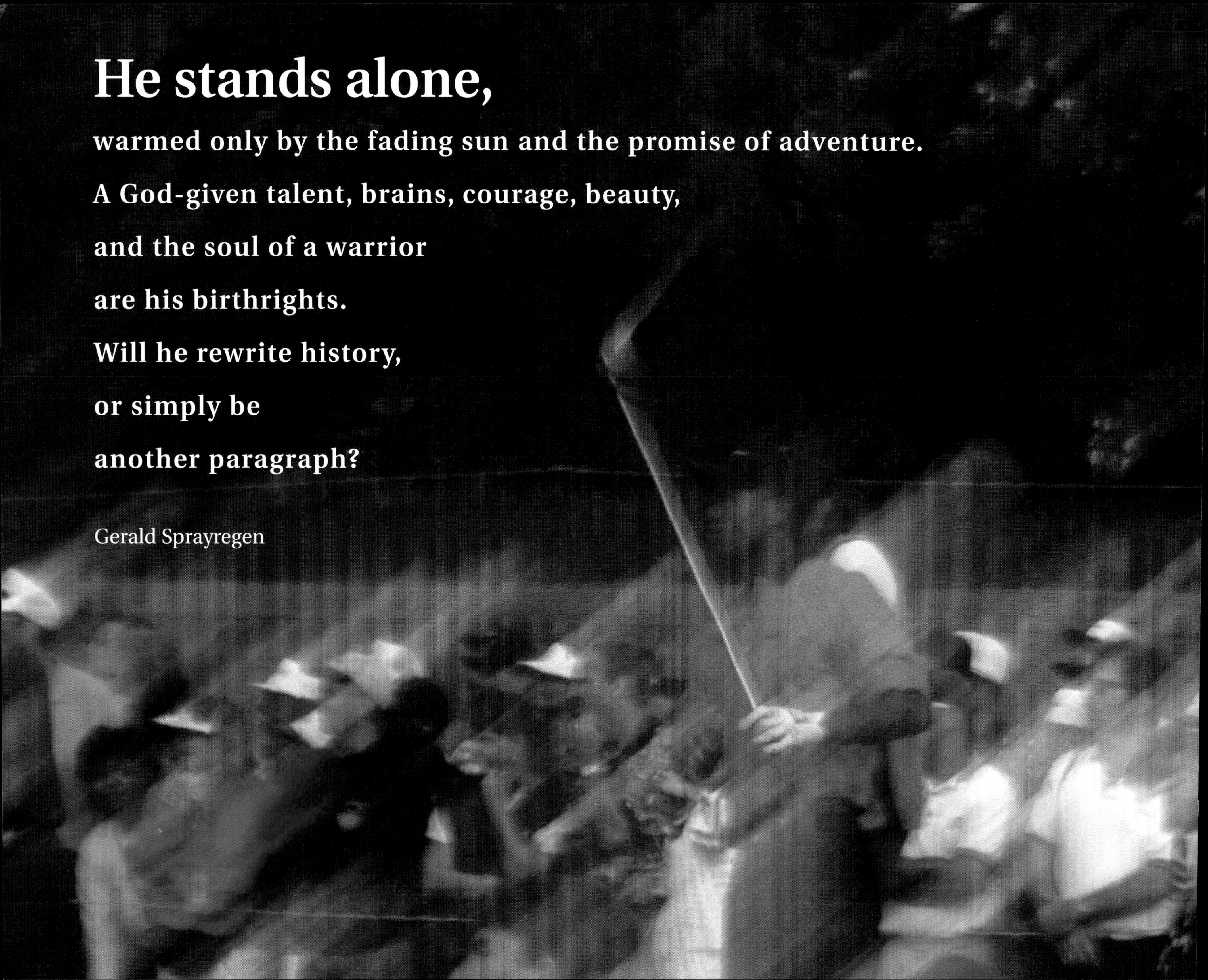

A thousand fans follow his every move.

"Get legs," they yell, when his pitch lands softly on the green, and rolls . . .

"Get going . . . hurry."

The ball lips out. They groan. Tiger casts a skyward glance.

"Tough break," they murmur. ***"Get 'em on the next hole,"*** they shout.

But when his shadow disappears from the green,
and there's only that image frozen in their imaginations,
they relish the minor tragedy of the moment, the thwarted goal.
They understand it, like ancient Greeks watching from a green hillside
while a king falters, as they themselves do.

William Hallberg

I like the feeling of trying my hardest

under pressure . . .

But it's so intense, *it's hard to describe.*

It feels like a lion is tearing at my heart.

Tiger Woods

The first time I saw Jack Nicklaus or Arnold Palmer or Ben Hogan or Sam Snead or Lee Trevino, I saw something special.

As soon as I saw Tiger Woods swing today,

I thought, man, this young guy has got it.

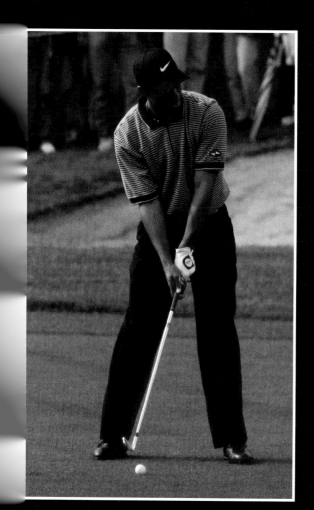

"It" is something indescribable.

It's the way he puts his hands on the club, the way he stands over the ball.

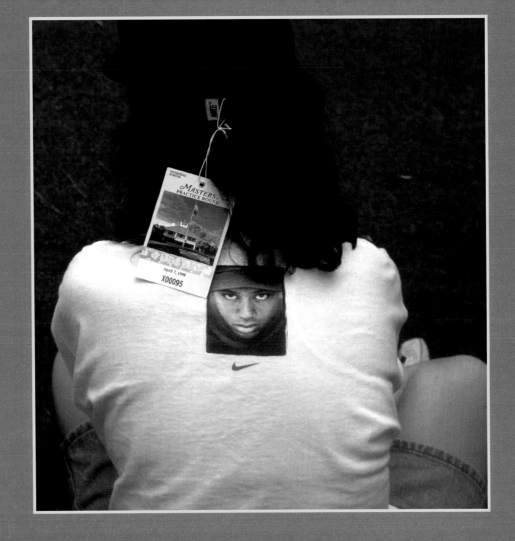

I like the idea of being
a role model.

It's an honor.
People took the time to help me as a kid,
and they impacted my life.
I want to do the same for kids.

Tiger Woods

My dad,

in essence, is the fairway.

I am like the wild grass

that begins at its edges

and moves off

into deeper rough.

Jeff Wallach

My son

becomes the man

I might have been,

had the world

been different

way back when.

How wistful

to imagine

my younger self,

walking these fairways,

arcing nine irons

stiff to the pin,

tapping in for birdie.

The crowd cheers;

he waves to them

for both of us.

William Hallberg

Golf is the most personal of games.

Only you can make the shots,

and the consequences fall upon you

and you alone.

How odd then to feel the weight of a

nation's hopes upon your shoulders,

and the burden of expectations

from the members of your team.

You must ignore them for the moment.

Let the red of their shirts, and their golf bags

colored like Old Glory,

meld into the background.

You must focus instead

on a pyramid of white golf balls,

which have assumed

the molecular structure of fear.

Your job is to disassemble them and hurl

the atoms one by one into space until there is only

the familiar green turf to contend with.

William Hallberg

I'm very happy with his progress.

The tough part is that every time he plays in a tournament, no matter what it is, he's expected to win. No one is going to win every time out. As he's gotten better,

I think he's feeling a little of the pressure

The morning dew

lay siege,

creating whispers

from his tireless fans,

while both are muted

by the encroaching dawn,

as **Butch***,*

hands in pockets,

watches silently.

Gerald Sprayregen

S ometimes it's hard to remember
that I'm calling the shots . . .
B utch has already told me
I have to be strong enough to say no
and tell people who are working for me
what to do, including him.
I n a way I've gone from being
a college sophomore to a mini-CEO.
I t's kind of hard.
I mean, I'm 20 years old . . .

Tiger Woods, 1995

In golf,
we see reflections of ourselves.
The best and worst we are
look back at us.
A fickle breeze
makes fools
of us.
Or heroes.
Or something
in between.

William Hallberg

"One day you're going to grow up

and then you're going to be me." . . .

He picked up a long stick

and put it in my hand.

Then he showed me the backswing.

"You've got to know one thing

to drive a golf ball,"

he told me,

"and that's that the club is part of you. . . .

The club is your hand. . . .

It's your bone.

It's your whole arm

and your skeleton

and your heart."

Ethan Canin

Unfortunately, you also see
the possibility of failure
every time you look at the ball,
sitting there so innocuously.
Your pain is assured. So is the illusion—or the belief—
that you can succeed.
The only way to play the game
is to play it one shot at a time.
Every shot offers the possibility of success,
of immediate reward.
And every shot offers
the possibility of failure as well.

Lorne Rubenstein

Arnold [Palmer] and I agree that you could take his Masters and my Masters and add them together, and this kid should win more than that.

Jack Nicklaus

The big levers and powerful engines of the perfect swing depend upon the tender caress of hands upon the leather grip.

His delicate, sensitive fingers contradict the swing's imposing armature.

They refine it, define it, bring it toward perfection.

William Hallberg

*W*hat Michael Jordan did for basketball,
Tiger absolutely can do for golf.

Phil Knight
Nike CEO

Marriages have started,
ended,
and restarted
in the time it takes Woods
to line up a putt.

John Feinstein

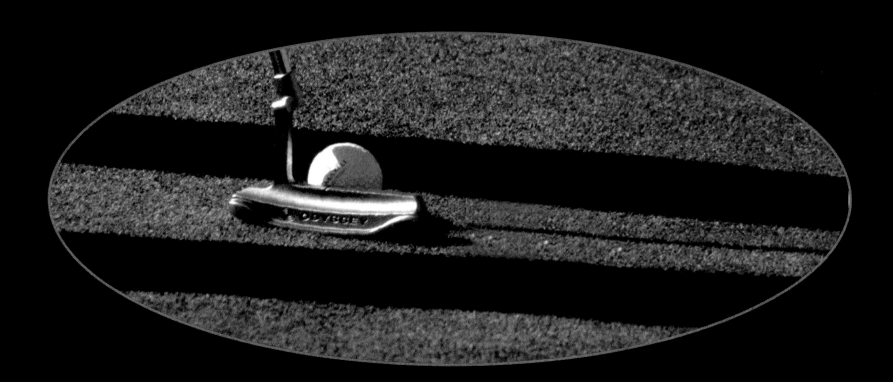

I've always studied great players.

I like to find out

why they were great.

I've never tried

to emulate one person.

I've tried to adopt the best

attributes of many people.

I like to study their decision-making on the golf course . . . to make one super player.

Tiger Woods

I used to love to watch Tom Watson putt, Trevino hit little wedges, or Nicklaus hit long irons.

Jack Nicklaus, Arnie Palmer, Tom Watson
move gracefully across the corridors of time

and still have the capacity to defeat infidels who unceremoniously challenge their supremacy.

Effortlessly, a new potential titan has thrown down the gauntlet,

and his entourage has proclaimed the golfing kingdom as their own.

Only with the passage of years and many more Masters

will we be able to determine if his crown was made of gold or papier-maché.

Gerald Sprayregen

She stood out, in a crowd of hundreds, all lining the path to the driving range
at **THE MASTERS.**
Her companions were a tiny stuffed tiger and the immense anticipation
she wore on her angelic face.
The moment of truth arrived.

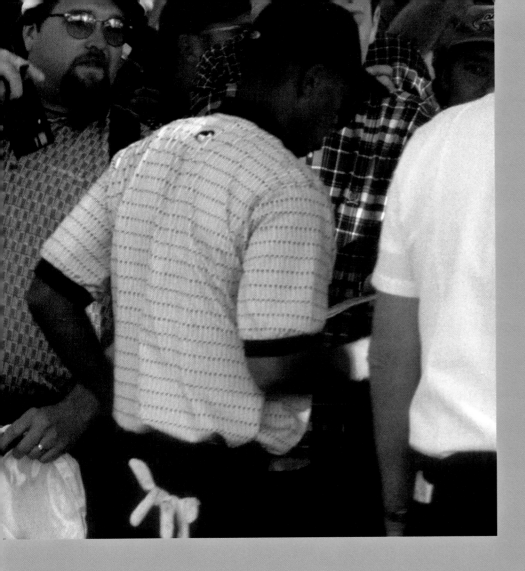 

As Tiger swiftly walked by, head bowed, he stopped, took her Tiger,
and autographed it.
Only a camera can recall the mesmerizing effect,
the thrill of that moment.
She will have a story for her lifetime!

Gerald Sprayregen

You can get close enough
to mastering the game,
to feel it, to breathe it
maybe, to smell it.
But you can't
master it,
not for a long time.

Tom Watson

On a sun-soaked summer afternoon when even golf is just itself,

if only for a moment, you can hear the rhythmic sound of irons clicking.

That cadence reassures the mind that golf, like life, abides a hopeful rhythm

that connects us to our bygone glories and to triumphs yet to come.

William Hallberg

the sharing
of the glory
with your
bosom friend
is everlasting joy.

William Hallberg

When your shadow's
longer than a flagstick,
and the crowd is
horseshoed round
the final green
to cheer you home,

Victory *is nothing if not shared.*

*There are no teammates with whom
the golfer can share his triumph.
In the wake of the loneliest of battles,
the golfer shares the ecstasy with his fans.
This is the moment he has craved in his isolation,
and its arrival is a glorious kaleidoscope
of color and clamor.*
"Way to go, Tiger," *they shout.*
He raises his fist.
"This is for you."

William Hallberg